MW00608944

Contemporary Gardens
of the Hamptons

M

Foreword by Alastair Gordon / Text by Thomas Christopher

Contemporary Gardens
of the Hamptons

LaGuardia Design Group
1990–2020

Alastair Gordon

A Sense of Continuity

Artists first came to the East End of Long Island for the light and rustic scenery: the sandy beaches, windswept dunes, saltwater inlets, and forests of wild holly, pitch pine, scrub oak, and shadbush. The Tile Club painters ventured out as early as 1878, and the rest followed suit, as did the architects, who came because of the artists and also the light, always the sea-brewed light. Peter Blake walked into Jackson Pollock's studio in 1950 and had a life-changing epiphany. Inspired by the performative aspect of Pollock's all-over paintings, Blake designed his own house in the shape of a pinwheel with sliding walls so that he could experience an uninterrupted, 360-degree panorama. It was all about the light and low-lying landscape of sandy moors, inlets, and bays, the "walking" dunes, pitch pine, shadbush, bayberry, and other native plants that grew on the windswept extremities of this 118-mile-long sandbar that was shaped by glacial deposits and hurricanes.

The postwar generation of East End modernists— including Blake, Pierre Chareau, Andrew Geller, George Nelson, and Gordon Bunshaft—saw their experimental beach houses as sculptural objects dropped into a watery Eden. They hardly touched the landscape. They might have planted a few Japanese black pines as windbreaks, but nothing fancy. They liked it the way they found it, but this kind of direct response was no longer possible by the 1960s and 1970s, when dunes and potato fields were filling in with summer homes in every imaginable shape and size. Landscape interventions became elaborate buffers and status symbols. Natural contours were often flattened or squared with paved driveways, privet hedges, high-maintenance lawns, and automated sprinkler systems. Something was lost.

There were a few architects who recognized the dilemma and attempted to soften the collision between nature and architecture through a more integrated approach. At the top of that list was Norman Jaffe, who envisioned his architecture as an organic extension of the land. In many ways, Christopher LaGuardia, founding partner of LaGuardia Design Group, has carried on that legacy and amplified our awareness of place through an authentic interpretation of the East End's genius loci.

LaGuardia grew up in a rural area of upstate New York. He studied architecture and landscape design at the University of Georgia and interned with M. Paul Friedberg, working on public spaces in New York City. He moved to Bridgehampton in 1984, where he worked for Peterson and Lynch, a landscape design firm based in Southampton. During those first few years on the East End, he and his wife, Jane, would set out on their bicycles and explore the back roads, peeking through privet hedges to find gardens and houses they'd heard about. This was when LaGuardia first discovered the houses of Norman Jaffe with their broadly sloping roofs and rugged stone foundations. In particular, he was taken by the way that the Perlbinder and Becker houses played off of their respective settings: one perched on an ocean dune, the other in a potato field.

"Norman influenced a whole generation of designers," said LaGuardia, who met the architect in 1987 and started to work for him on projects like Sam's Creek and the final stages of Gates of the Grove, an award-winning synagogue that imbedded a wood-and-glass structure within a grove of trees. "Norman always preached the poetry of space and light, and that was what we learned from him," said LaGuardia, who also found inspiration in the works of modernist landscape architects like Dan Kiley and Roberto Burle Marx, but especially the Mexican master Luis Ramiro Barragán. "Barragán did the most with the least," he observed. "He engaged with the landscape through his inventive use of walls and water." That has been LaGuardia's approach from the beginning, to extend the geometric volumes of architecture in sympathetic contrast to the natural contours of the land.

LaGuardia launched his own design practice in 1993 with a number of relatively small projects, including a terraced garden for a waterfront house in Long Beach on a barrier island off the south shore of Long Island. It was published in *Garden Design,* won an award, and led to a series of larger commissions in the summer communities of eastern Long Island. Over the next twenty years, the practice has gradually expanded in tandem with the general growth of the Hamptons, which exploded as a global

Top to bottom:
Norman Jaffe / Perlbinder House, Becker House
Luis Ramiro Barragán / Fuente del Bebedero, Jardines del Pedregal
Opposite: Christopher LaGuardia on site

destination and cultural phenomenon. Real estate values skyrocketed, and the houses grew exponentially larger, often filling their building lots. As dunes, potato fields, and forests were further subdivided, the art of site planning and sustainable land stewardship became more important than ever, and LaGuardia saw his mission as one of thoughtful mediation.

He had something of a breakthrough in 1998 when he was commissioned to restore the grounds of the Perlbinder house in Sagaponack, one of Norman Jaffe's best-known residential works. The original house was lifted from its foundation and moved four hundred feet back from the beach (a salvage effort that has become more and more common with the impact of sea-level rise). Instead of carting in truckloads of fill to rebuild the barrier dune, a freshwater pond was created, and the excavated earth was used to raise the grade around the house by seventeen feet. The reconstructed dune was planted with beach grass and extended northward to merge with an agricultural field. The flat expanse was reconfigured into a gently undulating topography, liberating it from the rigidly straight furrows of the former potato farm. Through this kind of restorative process, LaGuardia was both honoring his mentor and returning the land to its predevelopment ecology.

To keep pace with an increase in projects, LaGuardia's office moved into a larger space and expanded from a staff of five to fifteen over a five-year period. In 2015, two of LaGuardia's associates—Ian Hanbach and Daniel Thorp— were made full partners to keep up with the growing practice. Hanbach attended SUNY Syracuse and, during a year abroad, worked in Copenhagen on adaptive reuse and waterfront revitalization. He started to work for LaGuardia in 2005. Thorp grew up gardening with his mother in Worcester, Massachusetts, and attended Cornell where he studied with Professor Marvin Adleman, learning the art of grading and site design. He joined LaGuardia in 2007.

The focus of the LaGuardia Design Group's mission has been to merge architecture and nature through creative grading, planting native species, and stitching structures into the rolling contours of eastern Long Island. In some cases, the distinctions between architecture and landscape dissolve altogether and they appear to be one and the same. In the process, LDG specializes in negotiating and working with the many environmental restrictions that protect wetlands from pollution and waterfront properties from tidal flooding. "Somehow, we have to ground or anchor these large structures to their sites," said LaGuardia, who uses terracing and retaining walls to make outdoor rooms and create natural "vignettes," while playing with light, shadow, and texture. At one property, a dense underlayer of wild grasses was infiltrated with wildflowers rising up in brightly colored pockets to create a perennial meadow. For a historic property in North Haven, boundary hedges were removed to open up view lines and create a free-flowing sense of space.

"First, we study the site and try to understand the natural contours and plant communities before we do anything," said Hanbach. Wherever possible, the designers collaborate with existing conditions, as shrubs and trees are painstakingly preserved and recycled. At a property overlooking Peconic Bay, a venerable stand of hundred-year-old cedars was replanted to create a thickly wooded point of entry. A former tree farm in Bridgehampton was transformed into a bucolic residential setting by repurposing a group of mature Yoshino cherry trees and relocating them to become a shaded allée leading to the pool area.

Each project begins with the specific ecology of the site. Sometimes the land is reshaped and sculpted into a more natural state, as was done for an oceanfront property on Meadow Lane in Southampton. Here was the case of a pristine object—an austere, rectilinear box by Stelle Lomont Rouhani Architects (SLR)—set against the riotous backdrop of sea, sky, and dunes. Three separate structures, including the main house, guest house, and a pool house/studio, were artfully positioned so as to blend in with the sandy, swelling site, allowing each structure to inhabit its own micro-environment.

"You can't even see the pool house/studio from the main house because it's set fifteen feet below the crest of the dune," said Thorp. A wetlands area was restored with

From top: Oceanfront, Dunescape, Contemporary Compound, Sculpture Garden

waves of native bayberry while a selection of non-native species — including Russian olive and corkscrew willow — were salvaged and replanted. On the east side of the seven-acre property, LDG inserted a 74-foot-long lap pool — inspired by the pools of Barragán — that runs along a pre-existing pergola while shallow valleys extend view corridors out over Shinnecock Bay. For this project, the LaGuardia design team worked in collaboration with landscape designer Edwina von Gal.

For a courtyard house in Sagaponack, LDG worked in tandem with Barnes Coy Architects to create an artful matrix of perennial wildflowers and native grasses. A slightly elevated wooden bridge made from custom-milled slats of Brazilian hardwood penetrates a rust-colored porcelain portal and crosses the forecourt where the designers laid down a carpet of liriope 'Lillyturf' ornamental grasses. "It creates the feeling of a lawn that you'll never walk on," said Hanbach. A cross-axis to the central boardwalk was highlighted with bluestone pavers and flowering mazus. The house opens up to the north with an expansive parterre surrounded by perennial borders of Russian sage, asters, and wild grasses. "It's like a designed meadow," said LaGuardia, who established different ground levels with turf steps held in place by Corten steel risers. The steps lead up to a less formalized environment at the back of the four-acre property. Pre-existing trees were preserved wherever possible, including a weeping copper beech and a large katsura tree. Twin rows of honey locusts were planted along the western border in a long allée that leads to a tennis court and an open area designed for summer parties.

One of the firm's most challenging and rewarding projects was to reconfigure a relatively flat fourteen-acre site in Bridgehampton and transform it into an open-air museum. The world-class art collection includes major pieces by Walter De Maria, Richard Serra, Isamu Noguchi, Maya Lin, and others. Full-sized plywood mock-ups were made of each sculpture to help determine the best location. Each artwork was given its own context within the greater landscape and buffered from one another by carefully curated plantings, slightly different grade levels,

and allées of honey locust trees that effectively separate the property into eight different outdoor "galleries." Serra's Corten steel boxes were set directly onto a flat but expansive lawn, while De Maria's 52-ton granite sphere was positioned within a wildflower meadow. Twelve Noguchi sculptures were placed in a contemplative half-acre grove of ginkgo trees, koi pond, and a Zen-like pavilion by Richard Gluckman, while Maya Lin's *Lay of the Land*, a 385-foot-long earthen berm, was given enough room to undulate laterally across its two-acre site.

The Hamptons have changed dramatically since Chris LaGuardia started working there more than thirty-five years ago. The pressure continues to escalate with larger houses and congested roadways. The bucolic retreat that artists came out to paint in the nineteenth century is no longer buffered from the city by miles of potato fields and sandy wastes. It teeters on the edge of a suburban sprawl that threatens to engulf all of Long Island. Despite over-development, there's something about the landscape that carries its own memory — in the watery light, the bayberry and scrub oak — providing a sense of continuity. In their stewardship and respect for the native environment, LaGuardia's design team has managed to channel that memory towards a more resilient and enduring philosophy of design.

Sagaponack

Oceanfront

This seaside house designed by the modernist architect Norman Jaffe won awards when it was built in the 1970s, but by the time LDG became involved in 1998, the surrounding dune landscape had been washed away. The house had been moved 400 feet back from its original site and set into the middle of a low-lying corn field. The brief for the LDG team was to reimagine and reconstruct a landscape appropriate to a seaside setting and to fabricate a self-sustaining landscape able to resist the erosive power of the weather and a slowly rising sea level.

Calculations revealed that some 30,000 cubic yards of fill would be needed to reconstruct a protective complex of dunes and raise the grade sufficiently to provide a safe site for the house. The need for grade change was dictated not only by the damage to the dune, but also by a change to the house. In the re-siting, the building was expanded with a new master bedroom and garage set underneath the original structure. To preserve the integrity of the Jaffe design, the surrounding grade had to be raised to conceal the addition.

Rather than importing the required fill, the design team decided to "borrow" it from the site, excavating a 60,000-square-foot basin for a pond that varies in depth from six inches to eleven feet. This volume produced a pond that would function in a natural manner, and it yielded enough fill to raise the grade seventeen feet around the house and create staggered lines of east–west oriented berms that mimic, and function like, a natural dune system. To give the pond a sufficient sense of scale appropriate to the house and site, its margin was configured in a curvilinear "disappearing shoreline." Inspired by such famous water features as Capability Brown's lake at Blenheim Palace, this approach keeps the shoreline from being completely visible from any one vantage point. This ensures that the water feature does not overwhelm the view, while also suggesting that the pond extends farther than it does.

The house was anchored to the new dune-setting with a complex of decks that also hide the new construction. Newly planted with beach grass, the constructed dunes gradually descend to a rolling meadow filled with a mix of assorted cool and warm season grasses. The cool season fescues thrive in the spring and fall, while the warm season little and big bluestem and switchgrass provide summer interest. The pond was surrounded with native wetland vegetation and stocked with fish and aquatic plants. This planting provides a visual integrity, and it accomplishes the goal of producing a truly self-sustaining landscape.

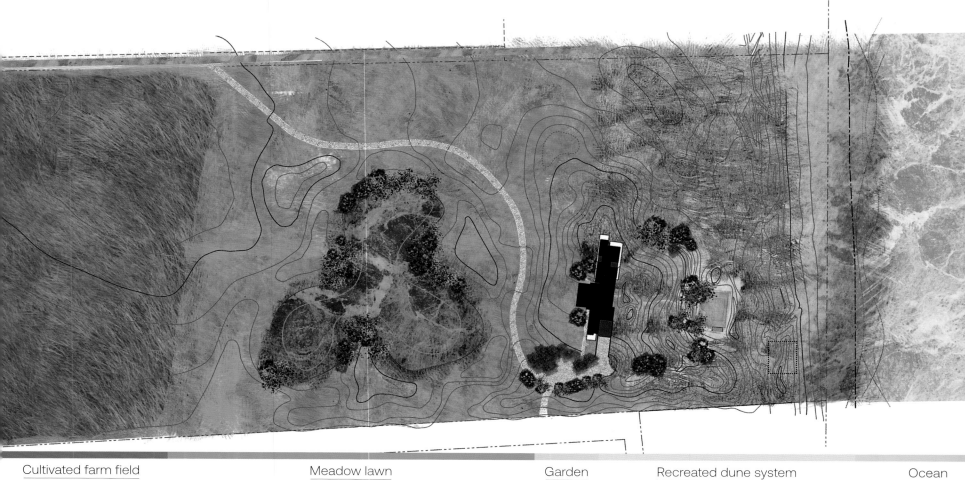

| Cultivated farm field | Meadow lawn | Garden | Recreated dune system | Ocean |

+18 new elevation   +7 existing elevation   +20 new elevation

Sagaponack

Farmview

Each landscape poses unique challenges. In this case, the primary challenge was the location: the two-acre site fronted on a busy road with lots of traffic noise. This was especially unwelcome because the client was a concert promoter with especially sensitive ears.

The response to this situation was two-fold. An acoustic engineer assisted in the design of a sound-reducing perimeter fence. The property was enclosed with a series of stockade fencing panels lined with a thick rubber membrane, whose foot was buried in the ground, and topped with sound-deflecting panels of plexiglass. This was hidden in evergreen hedges, which also function as a visual screen, closing off views of the exterior world and turning the newly quieted land inside into a very private retreat.

Although it diminished the sound, the fencing could not entirely banish it. To minimize the impact of the remainder, natural sources of white noise were incorporated into the landscape. London plane trees were added to existing mature specimens: their large leaves rustle audibly on breezy days. Likewise, a tallgrass fescue meadow was installed, which makes a sighing noise when stroked by the wind. Additional white noise is provided by three strategically placed fountains, one by the new swimming pool, another in an existing orchard of heirloom apple trees, and the third adjacent to a dining area by the house.

All these features were made to do double duty and contribute to a bucolic atmosphere. Except for a rectilinear panel of lawn behind the house, most of the property was given over to meadow traversed by mown paths. Beside the pool, an arbor was installed to provide shade and a gathering area. Terraces framed by luxuriant expanses of switch and fountain grass were disposed around the house to help translate the architecture into the landscape, and a combination cutting and vegetable garden was inserted into a gravel terrace.

The transformation of this property was nearly total. Even the existing house was demolished to make way for a new, contemporary-styled residence, and from the old landscape, only the orchard, freshly groomed, was preserved. What had been a standard suburban scene was reshaped into an elegant—and peaceful—country retreat.

Southampton

Cedar Crest

A creative reuse of existing landscape elements characterized this project. The clients tore down and replaced a one-hundred-year-old house with a new residence. Rather than start from scratch, however, in redesigning the landscape, an eight-acre plot on a bluff overlooking Peconic Bay, the LaGuardia team chose to make use of the century-old cedar trees that give the property its name. These were carefully dug and moved to create a cedar forest by the street through which the new curving drive wound its way. The ground underneath and around these cedars was planted to a native woodland meadow of tufted hairgrass. As the drive pulls up in front of the house, a more domesticated landscape was developed by enclosing the house with massed American boxwood and holly osmanthus shaded by specimen trees—a pair of mature-sized tupelos was introduced to supplement the existing oaks. Around this informal shrubbery border extends a softer ground layer of Pennsylvania sedge and fountain grass 'Hameln'.

A glass-enclosed, indoor swimming pool attached to the south side of the house furnished panoramic views on three sides and opportunities to bring the outdoors inside. On the east side, against the backdrop of the boxwoods lining the drive, a small Zen-inspired garden centers on a carefully chosen and placed specimen Japanese maple. Outside the opposite, west, side of the pool, lies a terrace, paved with irregular stone flags. Two irregularly contoured beds flank this, offering lush plantings of specimen sweet bay magnolias and specimen Japanese snowbells, under-planted with dwarf fothergilla, fountain grasses, and a frame of boxwoods.

Across a sweep of lawn to the west of the house, an outdoor dining table was set in a peninsula of turf extending back among specimen cedars that were brought in to supplement the natural growth. Thoughtfully placed to frame views of the bay, these trees create a savannah-like setting interspersed with drifts of native little bluestem and switchgrass. This wood and meadow landscape extends north to the crest of the bluff, where it shades into a naturalized buffer strip of beach plum and bayberry as the land falls away.

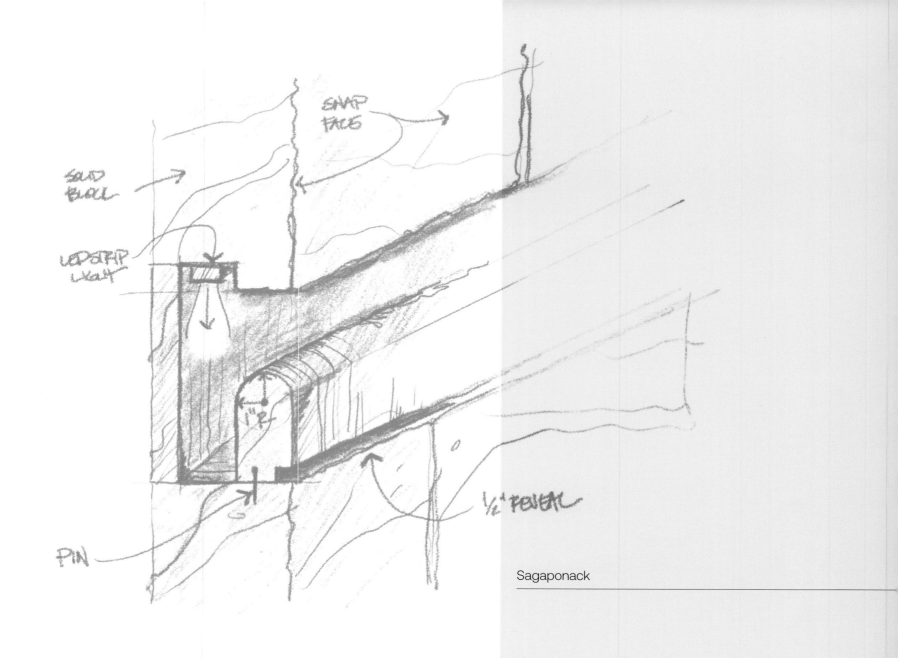

SNAP FACE

SOLID BLOCK

LEDSTRIP LIGHT

PIN

½" REVEAL

Sagaponack

Seaside

Superstorm Sandy was a disaster of historic proportions, but at least on this site it created an opportunity. Undermining an undistinguished existing house, the storm also devastated its landscape overgrown with exotic and, all too often, invasive plantings.

Redevelopment provided a chance to work with the natural characteristics of the site and shape the new infrastructure to reinforce the local ecology. A new house was built farther back from the beach. As required by FEMA guidelines, the house was raised above grade, creating the potential for a disconnect between the building and landscape. The first challenge, then, was marrying these two elements. The design team accomplished this by wrapping the house with limestone terraces that step down to the surrounding ground level. The buff-colored limestone echoes the color of the beach sand and extends the lines of the house, creating a strong visual sense of integration.

This theme of integration continues throughout the landscape. A new dune was created between the house and ocean as protection from future storms, and this was stabilized with a planting of American beach grass. Indeed, with the exception of a Japanese holly hedge by the front door, all the new plantings were natives selected for their appropriateness to such a coastal ecosystem. Shadblow, American holly, and black cherry were tucked into the slope running down from the house to a freshwater pond set back from the beach. Native shrubs such as highbush blueberry, inkberry, and groundsel were interspersed with native groundcovers such as Pennsylvania sedge and little bluestem grass, with grace notes added by specimen bayberries. The use of such indigenous species lends a visual authenticity to the landscape, with the practical benefit that these plants are well adapted to the sandy coastal conditions and thrive with little care.

Because of the dune that lies between the house and the ocean, the swimming pool and spa were located to the rear of the residence, overlooking the pond. Overflow edges in both water features transforms them into mirrors whose still water surface mimics that of the pond below, creating another visual link between the residence and its setting. A fire table fueled by ethanol provides a gathering point at night; covered with a tablecloth by day, it serves for outdoor luncheons.

NATIVE SHADS

BRIDGE

DRY
STREAM BED

Montauk

East Lake

The goal of this project was to link two adjoining lots on a hillside overlooking a lake. The clients had built two structures, a primary residence on one lot and a guest house on the other. LDG's brief was to join the two into a unified whole, while enhancing the environmental integrity of the landscape. The clients enjoy outdoor activities, including swimming in the lake adjoining their landscape, and they were committed to doing their part toward protecting its water quality.

The main obstacle to realizing these goals was a depression running down the border between the two lots that not only visually separated them, but also collected storm runoff. Rather than attempting to eliminate this, the design team decided to make use of and enhance this natural feature. Invasive plants were removed to free up the native vegetation. The depression was excavated, lined with a cascade of rock to simulate a seasonal stream bed, and then planted with sedges (Pennsylvania sedge), grasses (switchgrass and little bluestem), and other indigenous vegetation appropriate to the site. This constructed streambed now functions as designed, collecting water during storms, filtering it through vegetation, and eventually releasing it into a band of preserved wetland vegetation bordering the lake. The installation of a bridge over this feature connected the two lots into one and provided a link for the simple turf paths between the main residence and guest house.

One of the developing threats to the quality of the water in the lake is a high level of nitrates, and the clients chose to minimize the use of turf in their landscape to reduce nitrogen runoff from lawn fertilizer. Indeed, the only substantial expanse of turf is immediately around the swimming pool. Otherwise the planting was limited to mostly shadbush, bayberry, inkberry holly, arrowwood viburnum, red cedar, and other shrubs and smaller trees that naturally inhabit the area around the lake shore. By extending this tapestry over the two lots, the planting assisted in unifying the two areas into a single, environmentally healthy, whole.

Water Mill

Marine Meadow

Tucked between Mecox Bay and the Atlantic Ocean, this property boasts spectacular views, but it is also subject to stringent building restrictions on the ocean side. Because of this, the northern half of the property, the portion facing Mecox Bay, was the focus of the project. The original house was demolished, and a contemporary design by Stelle Lomont Rouhani Architects was constructed on its footprint. Between the house and the shore, the architects added a two-story structure accommodating an art studio and a garage on the ground floor and a pool house above. To connect the ecology of the shore with the interior landscape and to avoid blocking the view of Mecox Bay from the house, the walls of the pool house were made of glass.

FEMA regulations discourage adding fill to properties within the flood plain, but there is an exception for covering a septic field. In this case, the septic field is between the house and the new pavilion so it was possible to raise the level of that area to accommodate a swimming pool and surrounding deck with direct access to the pool house.

An adjacent parking area was set at a slightly lower level with a Corten steel retaining wall. This was surfaced with blocks set in turf to present a green appearance that would visually recede into the landscape.

The area between the house and the infinity edge pool was developed as a flowering perennial meadow so that the pool house seems to nestle onto a plain of grasses and flowers. Principally native plants were used in and around the meadow — switchgrass, bayberry, and red cedar. By introducing nature into the landscape this way, the line between developed and undeveloped is blurred, and the compact landscape acquires a spacious feel.

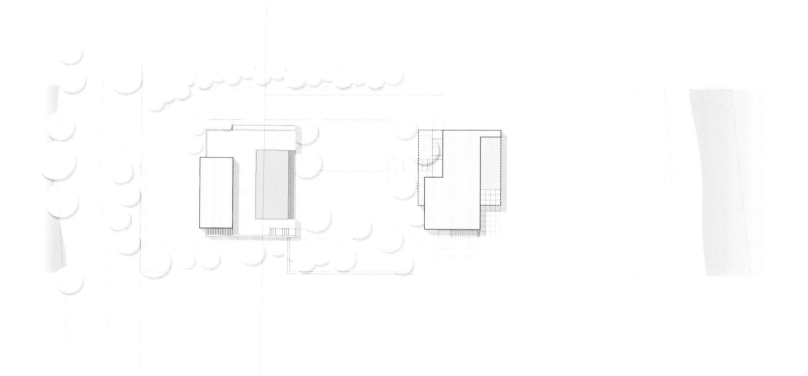

Water Mill

Flying Point

The clients' renovation of a 1970s-era house and their desire for a larger pool and accompanying amenities led to a complete reorganization of the landscape on this oceanfront property. The usual practice of locating a swimming pool between a house and the beach so that the swimmers enjoy a water view was not possible, even though the original pool had been sited that way. Over time, an increase in the dune backing the beach had blocked the view from the site. More importantly, FEMA and local building department restrictions prohibited expanding the footprint of the pool on the original site.

The solution was to move the pool to the back of the house, locating it in what had been the parking area. In this setting, the pool could be larger, and raising it eight feet created an ocean view through the trees. In addition, the new site was more sheltered from on-shore winds, providing a welcome and peaceful retreat for those who had spent the day amid the crashing surf and gusty conditions of the beach.

The clients opted for a Japanese-inspired aesthetic, reflected in the hardscape and landscape improvements that were developed as a simplified, modern interpretation of classical Japanese landscape design.

In the new configuration of the property, the road along which the approach is made is hidden by plantings of native vegetation. The arrival sequence proceeds from the end of the driveway into a carport, from which visitors ascend to an entry court dominated by a six-foot-high wall over which flows a sheet of water; this is the outside of the elevated pool, but the pool itself is invisible. A second staircase, a series of three rises and a landing, leads to the house, through a grove of crape myrtle trees. A turn to the right around a planter puts visitors in the pool terrace; framed in French limestone, this provides a view of the ocean.

On the ocean side of the house, twelve feet of sand were added both to reinforce the dune and to make the house feel more connected to the landscape and beach. A sculpture by Bernar Venet of weathered steel set into the top of the replenished dune helps to focus and frame the ocean views. Planters were installed to modulate the transition from architecture to planting. An oceanside seating area has a view of a meadow of beach grass rather than the beach. The sound of the surf, however, furnishes a soothing background to this serene spot.

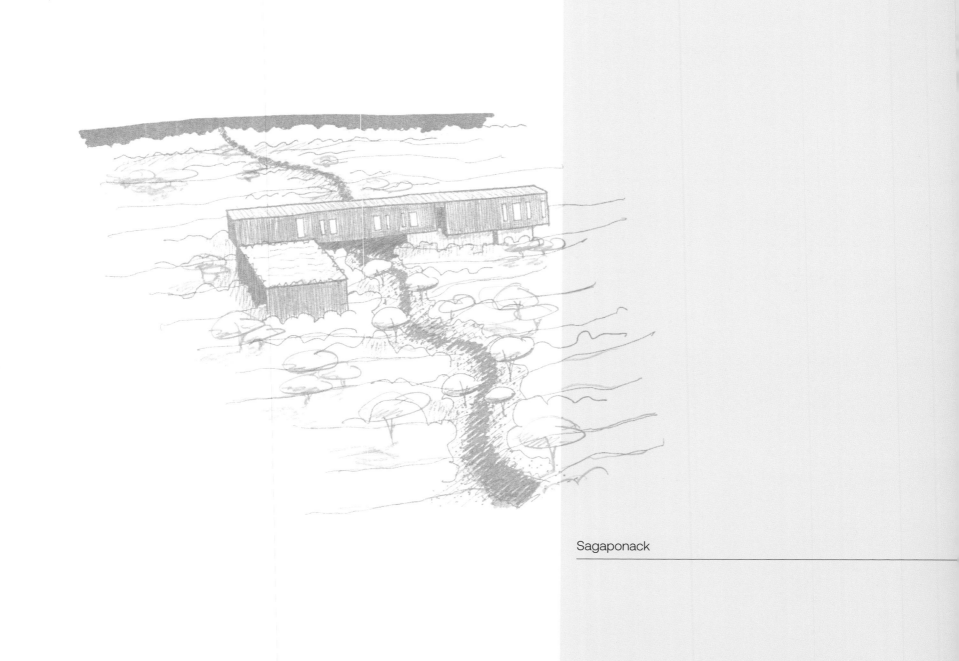

Sagaponack

Bridge House

The site of this proposed house, although scenic, required significant remediation. A four-acre expanse of former agricultural land, it suffered from a history of chemical and pesticide application and was a source of toxic, silt-laden runoff that impinged on the adjacent tidal pond. The architectural firm A+I and LDG collaborated closely to address these problems and create a handsome residence that is well rooted in the surrounding habitat.

To deal with stormwater runoff, LDG focused on embracing the watershed and turning it into an asset. Rather than diverting the water to the edges of the property so that it would run around the house, the design team decided to grade the land so that runoff collected in a central bioswale that would run through and under the house. Planted with native vegetation, the bioswale became the central feature of the landscape, creating dramatic views and experiences and connecting the house and its landscape visually with the wetland that surrounds the tidal pond.

The effectiveness of a bioswale lies in infiltrating runoff into the soil where soil microorganisms can attack and break down pollutants, thus cleansing the water. The absorptive capacity of this bioswale was enhanced by excavating its channel down through the existing clay sub soil and then lining it with clean sand topped with an eighteen-inch deep layer of a planting mix created by amending topsoil with sand and compost. The bottom of the resulting bioswale was planted with a ribbon of native Pennsylvania sedge, with the sides clothed in native grasses such as little bluestem, native shrubs, and small, multi-trunked trees. The visual effect of this planting is that of a wild, green "river" even when the weather and the bioswale are dry.

Any runoff that isn't absorbed by the bioswale empties into a 100-foot-deep buffer of vegetation planted along the edge of the tidal pond. Stormwater runoff was also minimized by keeping surfaces within the landscape absorptive. Even the parking area was paved with a permeable surface of blocks inset into turf so that the rainwater would soak in rather than run off. Similarly, the path to the house is set with pavers interplanted with steppable groundcovers such as mazus. The path rises as the landscape descends so that by the time the final bridge to the front door is reached, the visitor is up among the tops of the compact, multi-trunked trees, enjoying an uninterrupted view.

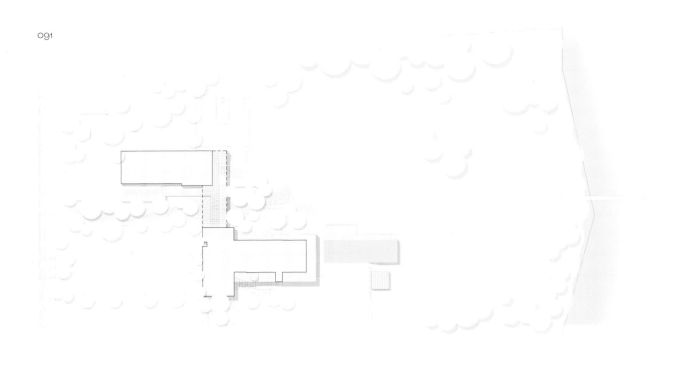

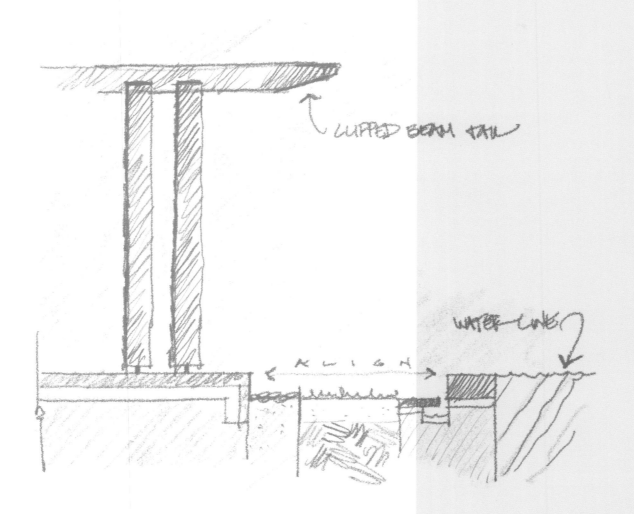

CLIPPED BEAM TAIL

WATER LINE

< A L I G N >

Water Mill

Modern Meadow

To integrate their new residence with its rural setting in a former potato field, the owners built their new house as a modern interpretation of a vernacular barn, and they allowed the surrounding two acres of grounds to lie fallow for several years. During this period, nature reasserted itself, beginning the natural process of secession that would re-clothe the site with vegetation and ultimately return it to upland forest if allowed to proceed undisturbed. In considering options for the property, LDG recommended that instead of starting fresh, the natural processes be reinforced and directed along an attractive and rewarding path. The clients enthusiastically supported this concept.

The first step was to edit the resurgent vegetation. Invasive plants such as multiflora rose were grubbed up and hauled away, and then the remaining growth was thinned and groomed. Next the design team carved out spaces for desired amenities such as a swimming pool. The effect of this process was to create a hierarchy of spaces moving from the architectural and constructed elements such as the house, the pool, and the associated arbor, to the green but visibly domesticated landscape treatment of turf, then to the informal meadow, and finally to the wilder vegetation that had grown up on the site. The borders of each of these zones were crisply demarcated, either by mowing or, in the case of the turf, by clipped hedges.

These lines created a subtle tension between the natural and man-made and also helped to settle the architectural elements — the house, pool, arbor, terraces, and steps — into their context.

Every effort was made to collaborate with nature in this project. Trees that were displaced by the installation of the pool were moved to reinforce the surrounding vegetation. The meadow was seeded with indigenous and naturalized grass species, such as fescues, little bluestem, and switchgrass. The inclusion of both cool season grasses (the fescues), which make peak growth during the spring and fall, and warm season grasses (the little bluestem and switchgrass), ensured that the meadow would remain vigorous and attractive throughout the growing season.

Architectural elements were treated sculpturally. The rim-flow pool is parallel to the axis of the house, and its edge is elevated to emphasize the mirror-like quality of the water. The flanking pool arbor was styled to match that running along the back of the house. The hard, rectilinear edges of these features contrast strongly with the flow of the surrounding meadow with its punctuating clumps of self-sown trees and shrubs. Nature, if left to its own process of succession, is never static. As a result, the wilder areas of this landscape will continue to evolve, subtly changing the experience of it over time.

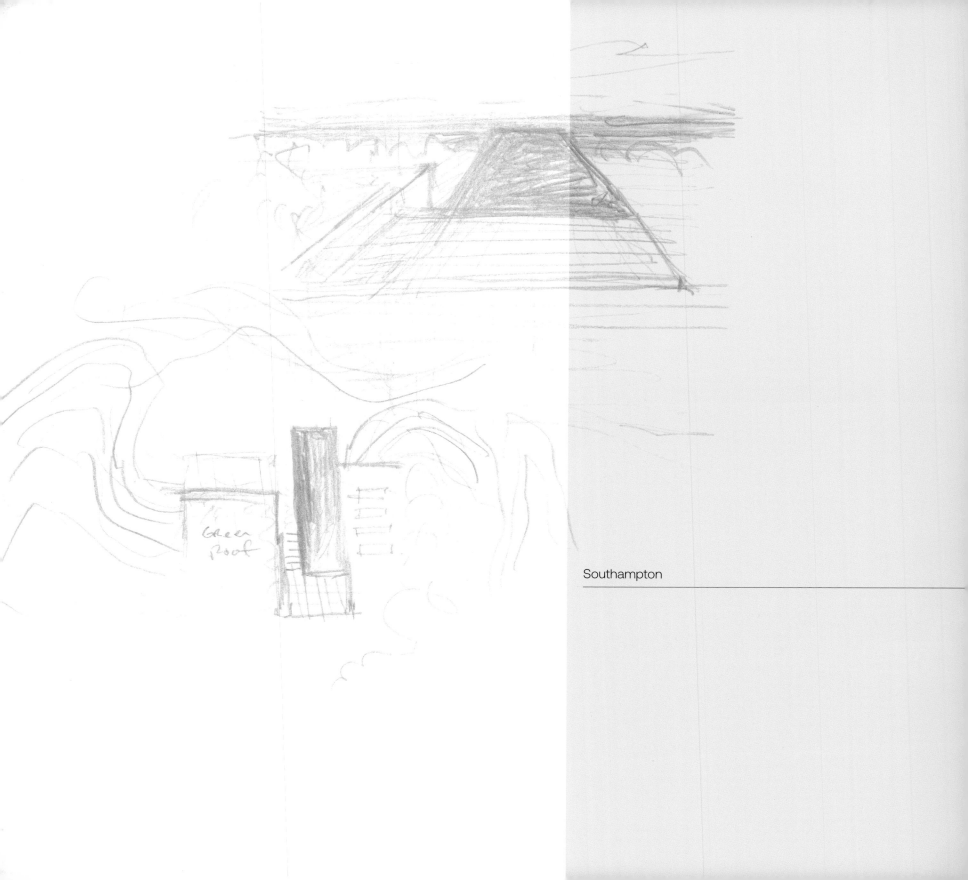

Green
Roof

Southampton

Dunescape

Sometimes the most attractive settings come with serious challenges. This pristine site, for example, is nestled into a heavily protected natural dune system that is home to uncommon native species of plants and animals. Even walking on the dunes is prohibited. As a result, only 20 percent of the lot was open to development, and the rest had to remain untouched. To keep the built landscape from seeming constricted and out of scale with the house, it had to be integrated seamlessly into its natural surroundings so that there was a sense of uninterrupted flow.

The LDG design team accomplished this by using only indigenous plants common in the dune system. The dune vegetation was extended into the landscaped area by laying down swathes of American beach grass, bearberry, and beach heather over the sandy soils at the perimeter. To organize the landscape and create a sense of shelter around the house, the designers relied on native shrubs and trees such as beach plum, bayberry, shadblow, and American holly. Using plants native to the setting also eliminated the need for amending the soil and relying on heavy irrigation.

The transition from house to pool is a broad rectangular deck of naturally weathered wood, and the pool itself was sculpted as a raised black plinth. To soften what could be a severe space, the adjacent terrace was paved with irregularly shaped flagstones laid dry so that drought-resistant sedums could be planted into joints. The portion of the pool enclosure abutting the reserve area is a low palisade of rectangular steel pickets, which were sand-blasted so that they would acquire a patina of red-brown rust and merge visually with the browns of the natural background.

Ornamentation had to be sparing in this understated setting. A border of purple-flowered catmint 'Walker's Low' lines the walk along the south side of the house; carefully placed shadblows mark the entrances. Great restraint, combined with a deft touch and a special vision of the plantings, has produced a landscape that harmonizes with the surrounding dune system.

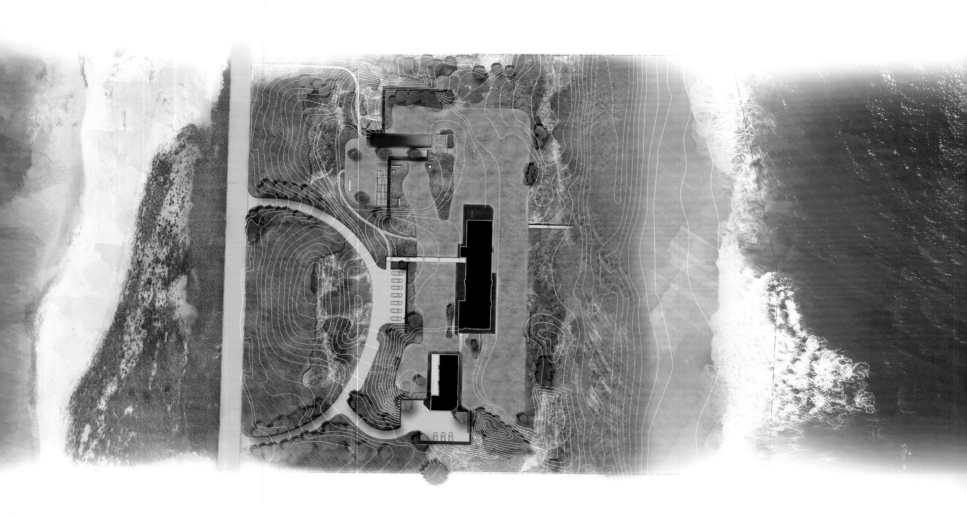

CRAPE
MYRTLE

LOW WATER

ROUND TABLE

CHAIR

HOUSE

3'

Water Mill

Longview

Located on two acres of a former horse farm, this house and landscape include references to the site's past in such details as the surrounding paddock-style fencing. These features lend the residence an air of rusticity, as well as integrating the landscape with the still active polo ground and horse paddocks that are its view across the road.

The design group also enhanced the landscape's rustic appearance with both the planting and the hardscape. Fescue meadows flourish around the property's perimeter, and a tousled but disciplined expanse of shorter native grasses — prairie dropseed and wavy hair grass — frames the front entry way of the house in a refined reference to the pasture that formerly occupied this site. A stone retaining wall and the edge of the swimming pool are both capped with a coping of snapped edge bluestone, again enhancing the rustic feel of the landscape. Instead of a diving board, the pool is equipped with a monumental diving rock, a slab of stone that was carefully selected and tagged in an upstate New York quarry.

Unlike many other retreats on the eastern end of Long Island this one functions as a year-round residence. For this reason, there is an emphasis around the house on evergreens, especially boxwood, which ensure year-round interest. The boxwoods, which embrace the foundation of the house in an irregular drift, have been clipped for a more refined look, and will, as they expand, merge into cloud-like masses.

This evergreen backbone is reinforced by the planting of trees and shrubs such as specimen blueberries, crape myrtles, and a spectacular copper beech whose strong and distinctive branching structure and textural barks will emerge to display their beauty during the colder months when the foliage has fallen away. Including winterberry hollies in the meadows has ensured that flashes of red fruits will illuminate them when the grasses are dormant, as well as providing food for over-wintering songbirds.

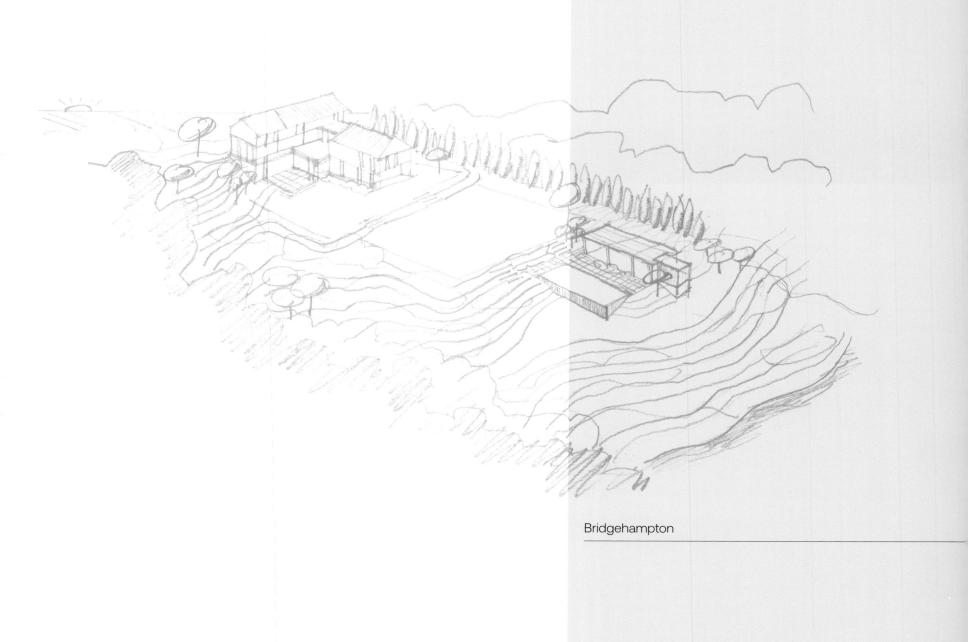

Bridgehampton

Hayground

Set on a long, narrow, three-acre lot between an equestrian center and a freshwater pond, this landscape descends approximately forty feet from the road to the edge of a wetland. The LDG design team was involved from the very beginning of the project, especially in siting the house. This was important because the constraints of the site mandated a sensitive arrangement of features that included not only the house, but also a tennis court, a sports court, a big panel of lawn, and then a swimming pool and pool house, before finally stepping down to the pond.

The integration of these elements led to the creation of a multi-tiered landscape with each "terrace" carved out of the site while still being very sensitive to the ecosystem of the pond. A buffer area of native plants, such as bayberry, and native grasses was established above the pond, a precaution that not only protected it from runoff escaping downhill, but also repaired the ecological degradation resulting from previous generations of agricultural use. A narrow path winds through this vegetated buffer, giving access to a small beach.

The landscape itself had an expansive but low, horizontal aesthetic, with few tall trees. The house harmonizes with this, presenting a horizontal, earth-toned aspect that settles easily into its surroundings. The new design arranged several native tupelo trees around the house, not only to screen views of neighbors and enhance privacy, but also to echo the naturally occurring tupelos in the surrounding wild vegetation. The rest of the planting was also principally native shrubs and grasses. The goal was to draw on the local wetland flora by the pond and pull it up through the site, allowing the landscape to integrate into its surroundings while softening the transition to the pond.

The driveway approaching the house from the road winds through a meadow-clad slope, creating an opportunity for sinking the tennis court and reducing its visibility. Behind the house and one step down in level is the extensive sports lawn. A step down from that is the wooden pool house pavilion and swimming pool. These are set in the best spot for viewing the pond and provide a peaceful getaway from the house, a place where residents can retreat for privacy and relaxation. The pool, with its vanishing edge, mirrors the sky and echoes the pond in the distance, helping to unite foreground and background.

Water Mill

Woodlands

Input from the client is, of course, foundational for every landscape design. In this project, however, where the client was a prominent interior designer, that input extended into a mutually rewarding collaboration on the details of the design. The vision of the landscape itself was strongly influenced by the client's perspective, for it became an exploration of outdoor living within the garden.

A number of strictures were imposed by the nature of the site. The house, a comfortable but relatively modest Cape Cod cottage, overlooked a wetland, and this dictated setbacks in any development on the property. On the other side, the front side of the house, was a relatively busy road, whose impact on the landscape the client wanted to minimize. This second goal was complicated by the fact that the site sloped markedly down from the road to the wetland, effectively elevating the roadway and increasing its prominence.

The erasure of the road began with the installation of a noise-attenuating fence along the property's frontage. The minimization of the roadway's presence was further reinforced by a feature of the swimming pool. The pool was central to the client's wish list, and it was accommo-dated by cutting a terrace into the slope with a finely detailed stone retaining wall. This wall also became the backdrop for a water cascade into the spa; the soothing sound of the falling water muffled residual traffic noise.

To enclose and shelter this central area, the LDG design team installed a woodland garden of ferns and hydrangeas on the slope between the pool area and the road. Here, a turf path meanders around mature trees that are lit at night to create dramatic views. A small orchard of dwarf apple trees was added to the front of the property.

The client's expertise in interior design expressed itself most clearly in the treatment of the area surrounding the pool. The placement of twin European hornbeam trees at the pool's foot gave it the appearance of a formal ornamental pool. A coping of irregular flagstones topped the pool, bleeding out into the turf with an irregular border, integrating the pool into its setting. On two sides, the flagstones extended out into a terrace that the client turned into an outdoor living space, furnished with a dining table and chairs, as well as a couch and armchairs, even floor lamps, surrounding a coffee table. An outdoor shower and changing area were hidden in the adjoining shrubbery. It was the client's inspiration to inject a note of color into this largely green landscape by painting the enclosing gates a periwinkle blue to match the door to the house.

Bridgehampton

Sculpture Garden

In this update of a classic estate, the clients retained the 1927 residence but commissioned LDG to completely redevelop the twelve-acre landscape. Notably, conventional features such as rose, cutting, and vegetable gardens were replaced with a series of tableaux to display the owners' extraordinary collection of contemporary art. For the LaGuardia team, the challenge was to differentiate the respective areas while still respecting the existing collection of mature trees and observing the owners' requirement that the views of the various artworks should not overlap. Full-sized mock-ups of the artworks were fashioned out of plywood and moved about the settings to finalize placement before footings for the bases were poured.

One exception to the rule of viewing only one sculpture at a time was observed. A monumental granite sphere by sculptor Water De Maria is clearly visible from the Corten steel boxes that sculptor Richard Serra created as a tribute to his late friend.

Distinguishing the different areas was accomplished in part by adjusting the grade. The swimming pool and surrounding area were sunken so that the view from the house should not be of the required, four-foot-tall surrounding fence. The LDG design team also deployed the plantings judiciously. Of course, the plantings also help to emphasize the themes and set the tone. A garden designed in collaboration with Edwina Von Gal, for example, which is dedicated to displaying works by sculptor Isamu Noguchi, is tucked into a grove of ginkgo trees which are remarkably sculptural themselves as well as conveying an Asiatic theme. The pavilion that provides weather-safe viewing for this area, is fashioned from Alaskan cedar connected with an intricate Japanese-inspired joinery that includes no metal fasteners.

The planting serves pragmatic purposes as well. The De Maria sphere is set on the apex of a mounded wildflower meadow that drains on all sides into rain gardens planted with moisture-loving natives such as swamp white oaks and witch hazel. One of the most challenging, but also fascinating, parts of this project was the creation of *Lay of the Land*, a landform sculpture by Maya Lin. This sinuous, 385-foot long sculpture was created not once, but twice. First, it was painstakingly mocked up with waste soil, and carefully measured as a drainage plan was worked out. Then the full-sized model was removed and the final installation assembled, complete with drainage, precisely to the measurements and sodded. Art is not only intrinsic to this landscape; at least in this instance, it is the landscape.

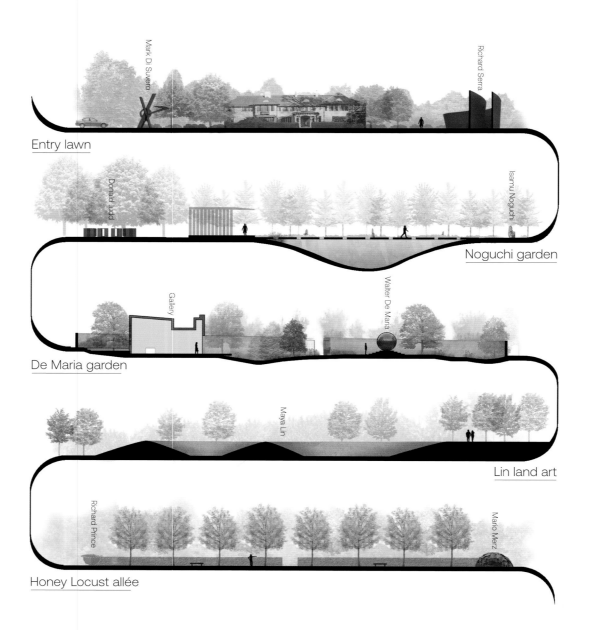

Entry lawn

Mark Di Suvero

Richard Serra

Noguchi garden

Donald Judd

Isamu Noguchi

De Maria garden

Gallery

Walter De Maria

Lin land art

Maya Lin

Honey Locust allée

Richard Prince

Mario Merz

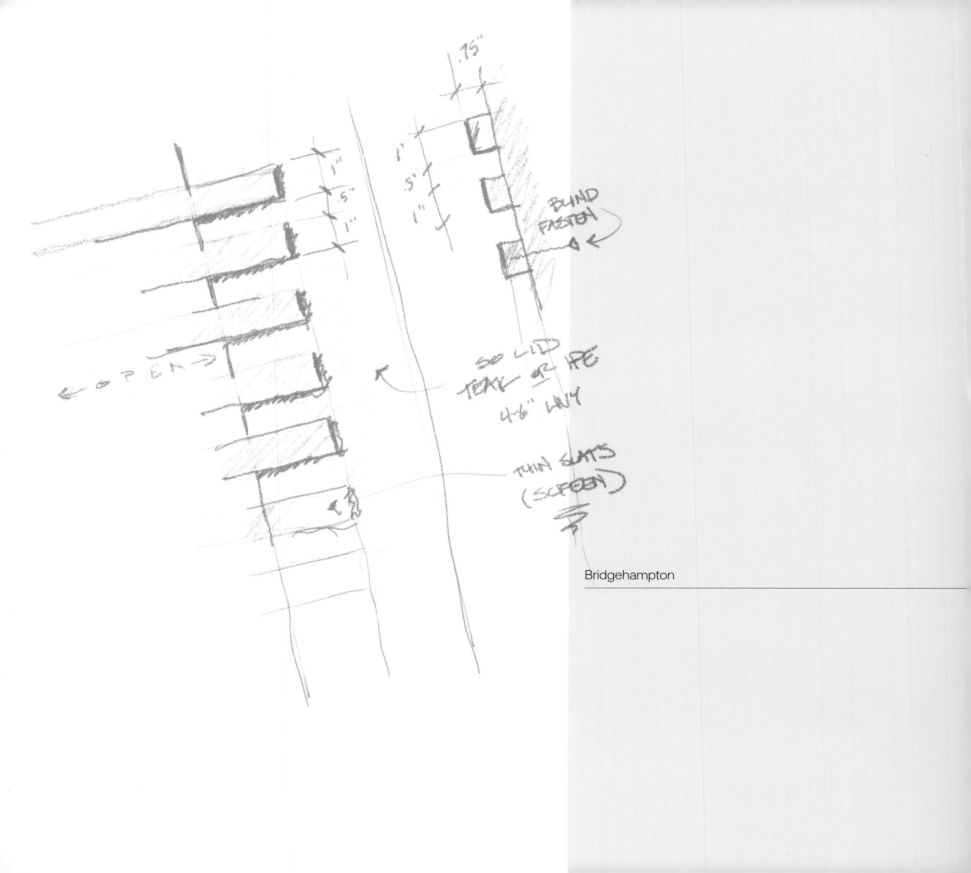

.75"

1"
5"
1"

1"
5"
1"

BLIND
FASTEN

SOLID
TEAK or IPE
4-6" WИY

THIN SLATS
(SCREEN)

Bridgehampton

Country Garden

Originally part of a larger property, this parcel of land included a former working nursery that was preserved as an agricultural area, albeit no longer as an active business. The client wished to open a view of its mature plantings from the new residential landscape, essentially practicing a design strategy known as "borrowing landscape." By including references to the landscape beyond his own, he could erase the division between the two.

Honoring the history of the landscape made sense, but it also challenged the ingenuity of the LDG design team. The residence, an existing house, is situated at a high point that provides outstanding views of the trees planted in the nursery twenty years ago. The strong linear nature of the plantings, arranged in parallel straight rows typical of a nursery, informed the design of the new residential landscape. The swimming pool, a custom rim-flow pool, is long and relatively narrow and set on the same axis as the nursery planting, creating a connection between it and the landscape beyond. The view from inside the pool is down the space framed by two former nursery rows. A custom ipe arbor on a stone plinth was set above the pool terrace, inviting for dining and socializing.

The variety of gardens created throughout the property provided more links to the past since they relied heavily on plants that were growing within the nursery. In this way, parallel rows of Yoshino cherry trees were converted into an allée framing a path, while parallel rows of fastigiate beeches became a backdrop for the pool arbor. In all, some forty of the existing trees were re-purposed within the newly designed landscape.

New plantings were interwoven with the plants transplanted out of the nursery. Rectilinear panels of fountain grass were inset with the cinnamon, clustered trunks of white-flowering 'Natchez' crape myrtles to soften the pool area. These also became a feature of the amphitheater-like surround of a sunken tennis court, in this instance creating a more tailored effect as they were dotted into a groundcover of liriope. Through the planting and the echoing of themes throughout the property, an integration of the new residential landscape with the preserved nursery was achieved and that line between the two blurred.

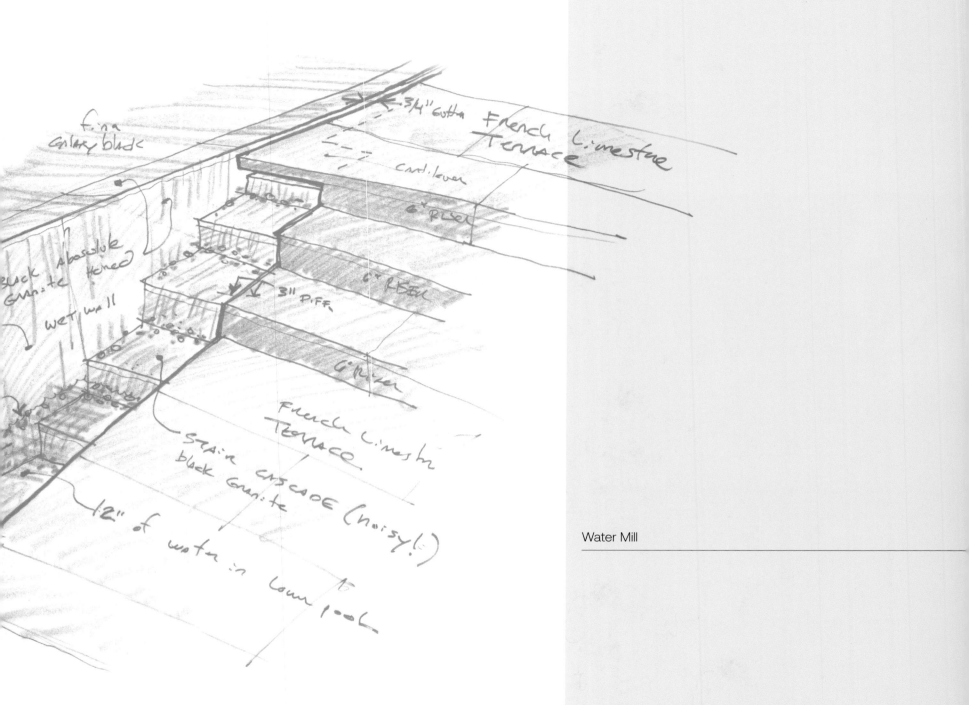

fine
Galaxy black

Black Absolute
Granite Honed

wet wall

3/4" Gutter French Limestone
Terrace

Cantilever

6" Riser

6" Riser

3" Diff.

6" Riser

French Limestone
Terrace

Stair Cascade (noisy!)
black Granite

12" of water in lower pool

Water Mill

Village Garden

This property belongs to an art collector who wanted to transform the landscape into an outdoor gallery for his collection of minimalist sculpture, which includes works by Masatoshi Izumi, Tony Cragg, John Chamberlain, and many others.

The program began with a clean sweep of the existing, overgrown landscaping; all that was left were the trees. Then the site was encircled with a clipped Leyland cypress hedge. The enclosed space was treated sculpturally to create a series of controlled and visually calm settings for the individual artworks. At the same time, care was taken to include enough interest in the various areas to accent the art displays. So, for example, a fountain adds a peaceful ambience to a sunken courtyard off the house, where climbing hydrangea clothes a wall, and a bonsai, a miniature grove of meticulously trained trees, crowns a table. Each sculpture is curated to a specific setting, and these were arranged so that the scenes do not overlap.

Clean lines, monolithic forms, and natural materials define this landscape. Even the topography is treated sculpturally, with precise panels of turf set at different levels, balanced against creamy limestone terraces, all joined by flights of limestone steps and paths of limestone flags. Masses of clipped boxwood, eight feet wide but maintained at a height of two feet, were positioned around the house in another sculptural touch. The focal point of the landscape is a rectilinear vanishing-edge pool, which serves as both a swimming and a reflecting pool, the mirrored image on the water's surface ever-changing. With such a complex program within a relatively small space, it was essential to keep the garden within bounds. The garden spaces and the terraces are punctuated by clipped shrubs and compact specimen trees such as Japanese maples and a file of naturally trim fastigiate beech-es whose narrow profiles are further enhanced by regular shearing. Containing the plant growth is essential in this small and intensively devel-oped space, lest it become overgrown once again. The clipped and sheared shapes also echo and interact with the sculptures.

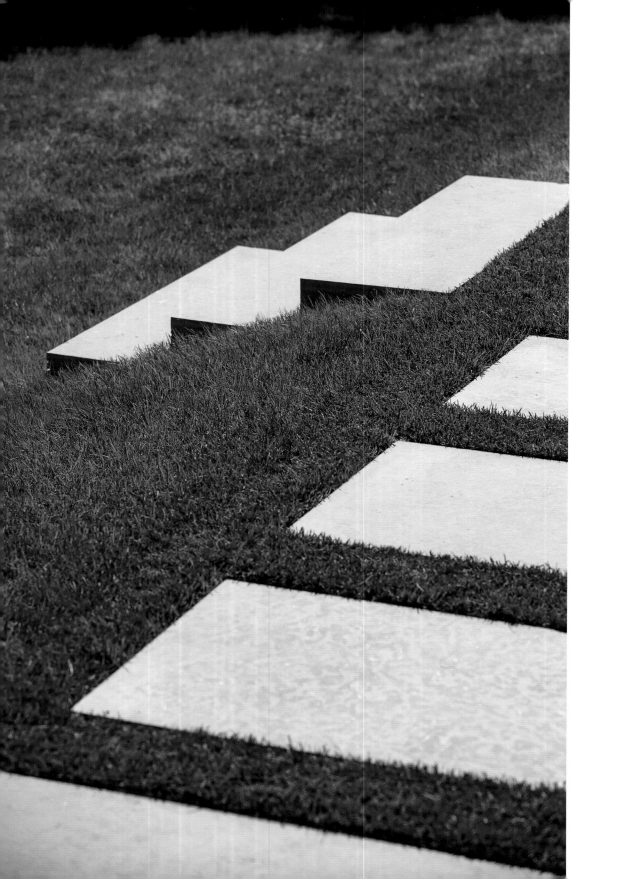
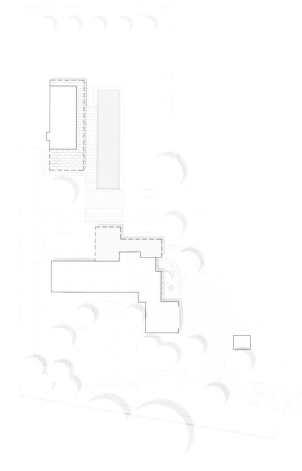

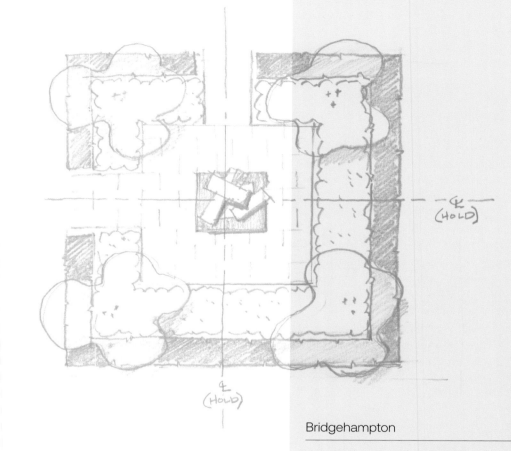

℄
(HOLD)

℄
(HOLD)

Bridgehampton

CRAPE MYRTLE

SCULPTURE

FOUNTAIN

BOXWOOD HEDGE

2'-0"   6'-0"   16'-0"   6'-0"   2'-0"

Mecox Point

Located on Mecox Bay, this two-and-one-half-acre parcel was originally part of a potato farm. One of the first steps in working on the site was to create a natural revegetation buffer alongside the shore of the bay to mitigate the environmental degradation of years of agricultural practices. One hundred feet deep and running along the shore for approximately 150 feet, the buffer was planted with native species, beginning with an underlayer of grasses — switchgrass in the low-lying areas and little bluestem in the upland ones — mixed with sedges. An intermediate layer of shrubbery — bayberry, arrowwood viburnum, and winterberry — was then worked into the fabric. Finally, the edges were planted with small trees, such as shadblow and black cherry.

The arrangement of the vegetation in this landscape was largely governed by the soil type; close to the shore, for example, the soil became boggy, calling for plants that can tolerate wet feet. As is common with former farmland, the site is fairly flat, which necessitated a careful handling of spaces. The parking area next to the road was left to turf, but inset with 4-by-4-inch concrete pavers, creating a more sustainable, water-absorptive surface that minimizes storm runoff.

Serving as a transition between this area and the house is an entry courtyard, featuring a bronze abstract sculpture set in a black granite reflecting pool to lend it extra presence. FEMA regulations required raising the first floor of the house, setting it five feet above the level of the parking area. The entry courtyard served to mediate this: instead of climbing a tall series of steps to the front door, there is a modest climb into the courtyard and then another short flight up to the entrance. The planting of this area is formal as befits the style to harmonize with the modern rectilinear geometry of the architecture, with orthogonal walkways, a boxwood hedge, panels of liriope ground cover, and a bosque of crape myrtles silhouetted against a clipped hornbeam hedge. A Valders limestone walkway directs guests around the reflecting pool and through the garden.

The nearby tennis court is at grade, but because the adjacent driveway ramps upward to enter the garage, the retaining wall of cream-colored stucco gives it the effect of being sunken. Capitalizing on the view of the bay, behind the house is a viewing terrace and, beyond that, a pergola.

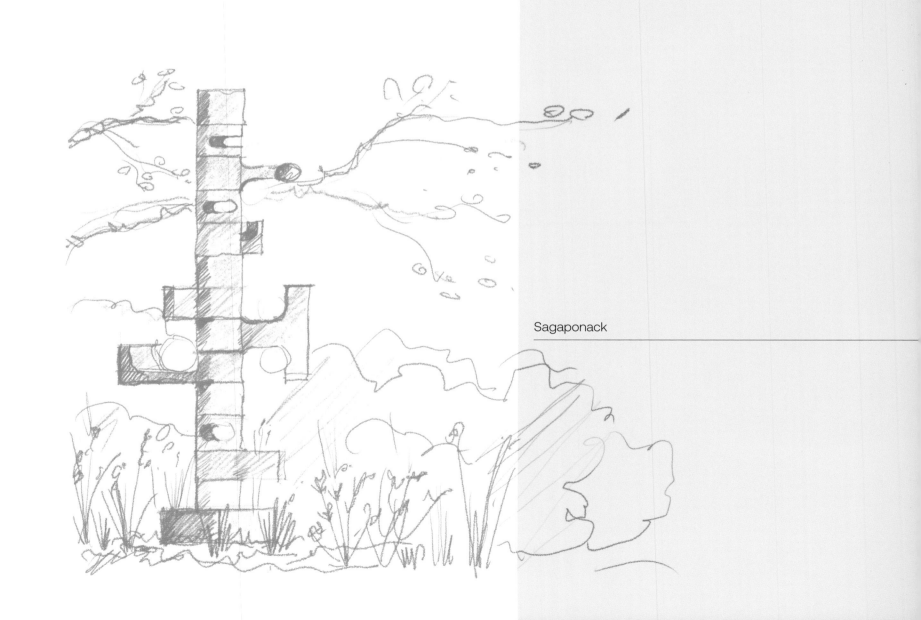

Sagaponack

Contemporary Compound

At first glance, this site seemed straightforward: a three-acre parcel that was relatively flat, featuring several randomly arranged mature trees, and all enclosed by a ten-foot-tall perimeter hedge of California privet. However, the architects Barnes Coy had a vision of bringing nature right into the house they designed. They set the stage for this by wrapping the rambling single-story house in glass. The brief for LDG, then, became to create interest on a relatively nondescript property that would give every room a compelling view to complement the architecture.

The design process started with the thoughtful location of key landscape elements: a parking court, swimming pool and associated amenities, a tennis court, cutting gardens, and gathering spaces. Subtle changes in elevation defined the spaces around these elements, forming outdoor "rooms." An outdoor seating area, for example, is distinguished and given intimacy by being sunken two feet below grade, whereas an arbor that provides a shady retreat next to the pool is emphasized by being raised an equal amount.

To reinforce this, a matrix of flowering perennials, including autumn moor grass, salvia, asters, and fountain grass, was overlaid on the landscape, not only to further define the spaces, but also to soften the edges of the built structures and generally enrich the landscape with layers of color, texture, and form. The existing trees were left intact where they could be included in the new design or moved and re-purposed when necessary. Thus, a mature weeping European beech was dug, with a root ball twenty feet in diameter, and moved from the center of the backyard to a position fifty feet to the east, where it could be integrated into the new scheme. The move also opened up a better view from the back of the house to a sculpture set into the lawn.

A notable example of the coordination of the architecture and the landscape is the view from a lofty and grand gathering room in the back of the house. This was given an equally grand prospect out across a broad panel of lawn. In contrast, the entry court at the front of the house, which is enclosed on three sides, provides a more intimate series of vistas with a planting of soft billows of ornamental grass in raised beds, backed by panels of liriope and a carefully balanced trio of crape myrtles. In this fashion, the goal of furnishing variety and interest to the eye at every window and through every season was accomplished.

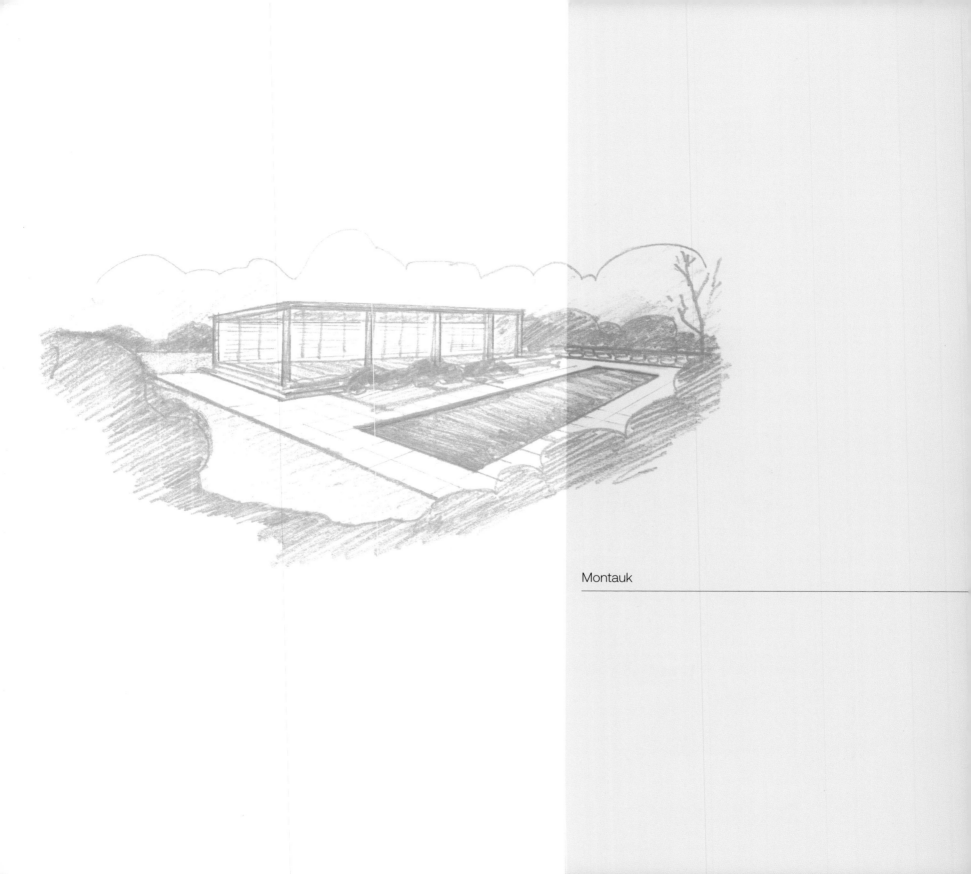

Montauk

Beach House

Although their residence is traditional in style, the owners preferred a modernist approach for the pool and pool house retreat they envisioned. This contrast suggested a physical separation, a decision that worked well with landscape setbacks mandated by the neighborhood association. As parents of small children, the clients also wanted to keep the pool area away from the house as a safety measure.

The pool house and pool were located at the far end of the two-acre lot, on a bluff above Montauk's Culloden Point, a dramatic site but one with extreme exposure to the northwest and the salt-laden winds that sweep in off of Long Island Sound. Salt-resistant materials and plantings were required. The outdoor kitchen is made of marine-grade, corrosion-resistant stainless steel, the decking is of ipé, and pool house woodwork of mahogany. The landscape was stocked with salt-resistant plants such as London plane trees, cherries, and crape myrtles.

LDG designed all aspects of the project, from the architecture of the pool house to the layout of the surrounding landscape. The goal was to create a space that would accommodate a crowd of guests, but also provide a cozy retreat for the majority of the time when the only users were the family. This was accomplished with a series of spaces, each one intimate in itself, but which in aggregate provided a generous space. The success lay in linking and balancing the various spaces. The lawn and terrace immediately around the pool are expansive, while the lounge and dining area sheltered by the arbor and the seating inside the pool house offer more intimate retreats. These spaces can be opened up to expand the capacity of the whole.

In the smaller spaces, elements such as light, materials, and detailing became critical. The setting was deliberately kept calm and simple, with a plain green plant palette, and luxuriously appointed spaces. Every aspect of beach-side living is provided for.

Southampton

Jule Pond

LDG was involved with this project from the beginning, collaborating with Blaze Makoid Architecture on the siting and placement of the house. Because of the sensitive nature of the site—a low-lying expanse of a former farm field bordering on a freshwater pond—FEMA regulations required that the house be elevated twelve feet above grade. In this setting of a vacant field, the structure could seem to be perched uncomfortably atop the landscape. The challenge was to resculpt and revegetate the land so that the house would fit in and seem to have always been present. At the same time, the clients were eager to preserve the views of the pond and the ocean beyond.

To root the 10,000-square-foot house into the landscape, the adjacent grade was raised by twelve feet. This enhanced the view. The swimming pool was placed to the side of the house to leave the vista uninterrupted. Similarly, the railing system along the elevated decks was custom built of vertical steel pickets with no cross-rail, to preserve the view.

Managing the transition from the parking area to the house was also challenging because the house was, on the front side, set twelve feet above the grade of the abutting land. Combining utility with aesthetics, the design team located the septic field between the house and parking area, using soil from the house excavation to overlay the septic field and create a gentle mound with shallow linear steps to negotiate the rise in grade comfortably. The design of the steps, varying widths of treads inset into turf, echoed a "bar-code" like system of fins used by the architect on the exterior of the house, helping to integrate architecture and landscape.

In the general treatment of the landscape, the goal became one of restoring and nurturing the natural habitat. A broad buffer of native shrubs and grasses was planted between the house and the pond to act as a filter for stormwater running off the site and protect the integrity of the pond's sensitive ecosystem. Turf was limited to the immediate area next to the house on the pond side, giving open access to the pool, pool-side arbor, spa, outdoor kitchen, and dining area. Elsewhere the site was seeded with native grasses to create rolling meadows accented with bayberry and other appropriate indigenous plants.

The design team inset a sunken terrace and fireplace adjacent to the front door of the house. Sheltered from off-the-ocean winds, it is the perfect spot to enjoy the spectacle of the sunset.

ARBOR BEYOND

FOUNTAIN

ARBOR | PLANTER | VANISHING EDGE POOL | PLANTER | ORCHARD

Sagaponack

Modern Retreat

Extending over a five-acre site, this garden developed over time: passing from one owner to another, the landscape had two distinct periods of design and implementation.

During the initial period, the garden became a personal resort where a bachelor client could entertain. The model was the luxury Amanyara resort in Turks and Caicos Islands, and LDG adapted the original's warm color palette of neutral beige mixed with natural woods and deep green vegetation to a northeastern setting. The plant material, while consistent with the richness of the Caribbean original, was revised to suit a very different climate and salty, maritime air as this property is only one house away from the beach. An exotic note was struck by setting Japanese maples on the peninsulas that articulate the swimming pool, while salt-spray and wind-tolerant evergreen and deciduous trees such as crape myrtles, lindens, and cryptomerias were used to shade and define the spaces into a series of linked garden rooms.

Organized around a central axial path, these are located toward the back of the property, deliberately detached from the house. Conceived as a retreat where the client and guests could spend a whole summer day, the "resort" included a wealth of amenities, such as outdoor showers and kitchen as well as a dining pavilion and lounge, sheltered by natural wood trellises designed in a Balinese style, each located in its own garden room. The swimming pool is large and was organized into different areas that open off each other, calculated to accommodate not just a single couple but groups of bathers. The spa became a separate destination, enclosed in its own leafy surround. The far end of the garden's central path was anchored by a heavy timber wood arbor that shelters a luxurious space filled with custom seating, fireplace, pendant lights, and a hidden sound system, which are shrouded by canvas curtains.

All of this was already in place when the property became the home of a couple with young children. While supportive of the original plan, the new owners wanted to add garden spaces nearer to the house, in particular features that would engage their children. A space next to the house became an outdoor extension of the living room, with sunken limestone benches surrounding a sunken central fire pit. A panel of lawn was transformed into a teaching garden with beds of vegetables, herbs, and cut flowers, together with an open-air dining area with cooking facilities, where the family could spend mornings and afternoons, even dine together or with a party on the custom-built table under market lighting.

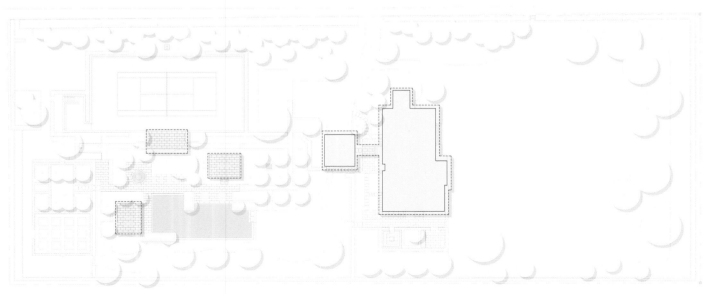

Acknowledgments

The making of a book that covers a thirty-five-year career is no easy task. Selecting twenty-one projects out of hundreds was a difficult starting point.

First, I would like to thank our editor Elizabeth White of the Monacelli Press. Elizabeth guided us so eloquently, offering experienced guidance on all aspects of the book. The many draft reviews made for lively conversation that I will miss.

Thank you to the immensely talented David Blankenship for his beautiful and original layouts, which make the book so refreshing and enjoyable to move through.

To Thomas Christopher, for his clear and concise garden descriptions that reveal just the right amount of information. And to my old friend Alastair Gordon, for his genuine and thoughtful introduction that reveals not only our firm's modest beginnings but also expresses the truly iconic place the Hamptons have become.

Within our office, this book could not have happened without the hard work and talents of associates Sarah DeGray, Thackston Crandall, Kerry Godfrey, and Amanda Taylor. They met every deadline, often working well into the evening, always expressing excitement at each review.

I also wish to thank all who work and have worked for our firm over many years. Without the collective efforts of all of us, none of the projects shown here could have reached the level of design and detail that people have come to expect from us. A big thank you to my two partners, Ian Hanbach and Daniel Thorp, for taking the office to a completely different level. I have watched both of them develop into very fine landscape architects and designers of the highest order.

Thank you to all the talented architects, interior designers, and artists that we have worked with over many years. The collaborative nature of our design work has developed many enduring and rewarding relationships for which we are extremely grateful. Thank you as well to all the engineers, consultants, contractors, and artisans for all that you taught us and for helping bring our designs to reality with the highest level of craftsmanship. The talented photographers that are included in the book also deserve a special thank you for their artistic eye and amazing captures.

And to all our clients who allowed us into their homes and supported our visions, we have learned so much from working with you and are incredibly grateful for the relationships we've built along the way.

Lastly, a special thank you to my wife, Jane, who has supported me both literally and figuratively throughout my entire career. They say that for every successful man, there is an amazing woman. I can assure you that is true. And to our children, Charlotte and Elliot, our greatest joy, who never complained once about play dates on muddy job sites.

— Christopher LaGuardia

Project credits

Oceanfront
Architects: Norman Jaffe; Cristian Sabella Rosa
Contractors: Kiwi Construction; Fort Pond Native Plants
Awards: 2013 National ASLA Award of Excellence; 2011 ASLA NY Merit Award

Farmview
Architect: Stelle Lomont Rouhani Architects
Contractors: SLR Contractors; Summerhill Landscapes
Consultants: SoundSense; Southampton Engineering

Cedar Crest
Architect: James Merrell Architects
Contractors: Aran Construction; Renner Landscaping
Consultants: Orsman Design; Inter-Science Research Associates

Seaside
Architect: Stelle Lomont Rouhani Architects
Interior design: Julie Hillman Design
Contractors: Seascape Partners; Renner Landscaping
Consultants: Inter-Science Research Associates; Southampton Engineering; Orsman Design
Awards: 2018 ASLA NY Honor Award

East Lake
Architect: Robert Young Architects & Interiors
Contractors: Men at Work Construction; Fort Pond Native Plants
Consultant: Southampton Engineering
Awards: 2020 ASLA NY Merit Award

Marine Meadow
Architect: Stelle Lomont Rouhani Architects
Contractors: Fountainhead Construction; Warrens Nursery
Consultants: Peconic Environmental Associates; KPFF Engineering

Flying Point
Architect: Stelle Lomont Rouhani Architects
Contractors: Wright & Company Construction; Whitmores Landscaping
Consultants: Southampton Engineering; Inter-Science Research Associates
Awards: 2014 HC&G Innovation in Design Award

Bridge House
Architect: Architecture Plus Information (A+I)
Designer: UNIONWORKS
Contractors: Bulgin & Associates; Marders Landscaping
Consultant: Peconic Environmental Associates
Awards: 2019 ASLA NY Merit Award

Modern Meadow
Architect: Harry Fischman Design
Contractors: Budd Webb; Marders Landscaping
Consultant: Southampton Engineering
Awards: 2018 East End Design Award; 2015 ASLA NY Merit Award: Residential Design

Dunescape
Architect: Stelle Lomont Rouhani Architects
Designer: Edwina Von Gal
Contractors: Bulgin & Associates; Marders Landscaping; MGD Horticulture
Consultant: Watershape Consulting

Longview
Architect: Arcologica Architecture
Interior design: Robert Stilin Interior Design
Contractors: Tom O'Donoghue Associates; Summerhill Landscapes; Avant Gardens

Hayground
Architect: James Merrell Architects
Interior design: Brad Ford Interior Design
Contractors: Cardel Development; Renner Landscaping
Consultant: Southampton Engineering

Woodlands
Interior design: David Scott Interiors
Contractors: Wirth & Company Construction; Landscape Details
Consultants: Orsman Design; Southampton Engineering

Sculpture Garden
Architects: Peter Pennoyer Architects; Gluckman Tang Architects
Designer: Edwina von Gal (Noguchi Garden)
Artist: Maya Lin Studio (*Lay of the Land*)
Contractors: Wright & Company Construction; Marders Landscaping
Consultants: Orsman Design; Blue Square Design
Awards: 2019 ASLA NY Honor Award; 2018 HC&G Innovation in Design Award; 2017 AIANY Design Honor Award

Country Garden
Architect: Peter Cook
Contractors: Hobbs; Whitmores Landscaping
Consultant: Shine Hampton
Awards: 2016 ASLA NY Merit Award: Residential Design

Village Garden
Architect: STM Design
Contractors: Lettieri Construction; Whitmores Landscaping
Consultants: Shine Hampton; Southampton Engineering

Mecox Point
Architects: D&D Harvey Architects; Stuart Basseches Architect
Interior design: Worth Interiors
Contractors: JBialsky Premier Development; Landscape Details
Consultants: Southampton Engineering

Contemporary Compound
Architect: Barnes Coy Architects
Interior design: Michael Rosenberg & Associates
Contractors: Webb Builders; Marders Landscaping

Beach House
Interior design: Ghislaine Viñas
Contractors: Landscape Details; Flawless Pools
Awards: 2018 East End Design Award, Outdoor Living Category;
2018 Luxe Residential Excellence in Design Award; 2016 HC&G
Innovation in Design Award

Jule Pond
Architect: Blaze Makoid Architecture
Interior design: Shawn Henderson
Contractors: Lettieri Construction; Marders Landscaping
Consultants: Peconic Environmental Associates; Orsman Design;
J.R. Holzmacher P.E.

Modern Retreat
Interior design: David Scott Interiors; Betty Wasserman Interiors
Contractor: Landscape Details
Consultants: Green Logic; Southampton Engineering
Awards: 2018 East End Design Award

LaGuardia Design Group

Alex Antilety
Barry Block
Alex Bluedorn
Elizabeth Borucke
Becky Brown
Noah Carter
Eva Cocco
Sam Coleman
Thackston Crandall
Josue Cruz
Sarah DeGray
Kerry Godfrey
Alexandra Grisanti
John Hamilton
Ian Hanbach
Steve Hatfield
Mark Hirschbeck
Matthew Horvath
Dean Janulis
Jason Kohler
Lee Krusa
Ron Kuoppala
Charles LaGreca
Charlotte LaGuardia
Elliot LaGuardia
Jane LaGuardia
Glen Lawton
Justin Leanza
Robbie Levey
Connor McInerney
Rambod Mirbaha
Lauren Moraghan
Joe Pucci
Holly Roth
Sydney Ramunno
Sarah Schlichte
Susan Simon
Amanda Taylor
Daniel Thorp
Kristin Trojanowski
Carlos Vargas
Grant Wellman

Current employees

Photography credits

Barragan: Armando Salas Portugal Photographs of the Architecture of Luis Barragan 8-9
Magda Biernat 87
Antoine Bootz 139-143, 229-231, 234-235
Matthew Carbone 107- 110, 114-115
Anthony Crisafulli 10, 11, 15, 17, 21, 29-37, 41, 43-46, 51-55, 59-61, 63, 67-73, 80, 82-83, 88-93, 97-100, 102-103, 119-127, 131-135, 148, 150, 154-155, 157-159, 167-177, 183-184, 191-192, 194-195, 201-207, 211-215, 232-233, 238-239
Pam Deutchman for Society-in-Focus 151, 156, 162-163
Rich Faron 185
Scott Frances 78-80
Jeff Heatley 23, 77, 82, 101, 181-183, 186-187
Nikolas Koenig 147, 151
LaGuardia Design Group 10, 153, 192-193, 196-197, 219-225, 239
Laurie Lambrecht 18, 19
Joshua McHugh 42, 47
Romantic Modernist: The Life and Work of Norman Jaffe Architect 1932–1993 8-9
Erika Shank 16, 22, 24-25
Eric Striffler 149, 160-161, 239
Kay Wettstein von Westersheimb 81
Robert Young Architects & Interiors 62
Sean Zanni/Patrick McMullan via Getty Images 111, 113

Copyright © 2021 Christopher LaGuardia and The Monacelli Press, a division of Phaidon Press.

First published in the United States by The Monacelli Press.
All rights reserved.

Library of Congress Control Number 2020951961
ISBN 978-158093-565-4

Book design by David Blankenship for Collective
Text set in Aeonik

Printed in China

The Monacelli Press
65 Bleecker Street
New York, New York 10012